CyberSmarts
STAYING SAFE ONLINE

Protecting Your Privacy Online

Bonnie Spivet

PowerKiDS
press

New York

Published in 2012 by The Rosen Publishing Group
29 East 21st Street, New York, NY 10010

First Edition

Editor: Karolena Bielecki
Book Design: Erica Clendening

Photo credits: Cover © www.istockphoto.com/Kristian Sekulic; p. 4 John
Kelly/Taxi/Getty Images; p. 7 © Rick Barrentine/Corbis; p. 9 Noel Hendrickson/
Blend Images/Getty Images; p. 11 © www.istockphoto.com//Derek Latta; p. 12
© LWA-Dann Tardif/Corbis; p. 15 © www.istockphoto.com/Jesper Elgaard; p. 17
MacGregor and Gordon/Photonica/Getty Images; p. 19 ©www.istockphoto.
com/Oleksandr Kramarenko; p. 20 Thomas Tolstrup/Taxi/Getty Images.

Library of Congress Cataloging-in-Publication Data

Spivet, Bonnie.
Protecting your privacy online / by Bonnie Spivet.—1st ed.
    p. cm.—(Cybersmarts: staying safe online)
Includes index.
ISBN 978-1-4488-6412-6 (library binding)—ISBN 978-1-4488-6418-8 (pbk.)—
ISBN 978-1-4488-6419-5 (6-pack)
1. Internet and children—Juvenile literature. 2. Internet and children—
Safety measures—Juvenile literature. I. Title.
HQ784.I58S665 2012
004.67'8083—dc23

                                                    2011018275

Manufactured in the United States of America

CPSIA Compliance Information: Batch #W12PK: For further information, contact Rosen Publishing, New York, New York, at
1–800–237–9932.

Contents

What Is Internet Privacy?

You can learn so much about different topics and people by using the Internet. If you are not careful, though, people can learn a lot about you, too. Make sure that you **protect** your Internet privacy. Internet privacy is the ability to control your personal **information**. It is about limiting what people can learn about

Even when you are using a computer in the privacy of your own room, you are connecting with a whole world of other people on the Internet.

you online. Why is privacy important? It is important because some people use the Internet to steal from or hurt other people.

You can protect yourself and your **identity** from these people. Keep your personal information, such as your name and birthday, private.

Internet privacy is important at home and on the go. Mobile devices like cell phones and laptops connect to the Internet, too. Be sure to keep these devices secure, as well.

Personal Information List

Sit down with a trusted adult and make a list of personal information you should never share online. Keep this list by the computer as a reminder. Remember the list if you use your phone to get online, too. Never post this information to any **profiles** or Web sites. Do not share it in chat rooms or e-mail, either. Private information includes:

- Your name
- Your age
- Where you live
- Where you go to school
- Your phone number
- Your e-mail address
- Anything else that can help identify you (like your school mascot or where you like spending time)

Creating a Password

A **password** is a code you create so that no one can see your information. Passwords can protect your computer so no one else can use it. They also protect your e-mail, chats, and many Web sites. The harder a password is to guess, the safer it is. A mix of capital and lowercase letters, **symbols**, and numbers makes a password strong. If your password is "sea turtle," try changing it to "s3a_TurT13." Remember and write your passwords down and hide them. Never send your password and **screen name** in an e-mail or share them with friends.

If you have a cell phone, you can lock it with a password. If you lose your phone, your phone numbers, e-mails, texts, and everything stored on your phone will be protected.

A strong password is your first defense. Pick a password that will be hard for others to guess. Your address, birthday, or phone number are not strong passwords.

Public Places Online

If you spend time in chat rooms, on **social networks,** or have a **blog** or Web site, you need to protect your privacy. Be careful not to post or share information where just anyone can see it. Some chat rooms and Web sites may ask for information you are not supposed to share online. Sites that people pay to join may ask for credit card information. Never enter this information without first talking to a parent. Ask a teacher or librarian to help you find sites that are safe and that protect your privacy.

Many sites have privacy policies. A privacy policy explains how a Web site might collect your information and what they do with it.

Sharing your thoughts and feelings online in a chat room or on a blog can be a lot of fun. Be sure to protect yourself and your privacy by keeping personal information off the Internet, though.

Privacy Law

The Children's Online Privacy Protection Act (COPPA) is a law in the United States that protects Internet users 13 years old and younger. This law makes it illegal for Web sites to gather information about you, unless your parents say it is okay. It also lets parents track what information Web sites have gathered about their kids.

Many Web sites have age requirements to sign up. For example, users on Facebook, the largest online social network, have to be at least 13 years old. Do not use a site that you are not old enough to be on. This is for your own safety. Privacy settings on sites for adults may be complicated or confusing. You may be putting yourself and your privacy at risk by visiting these sites.

Go online with a parent. She can help you find fun, safe sites and make sure you know how to be smart about your privacy.

Information in Your Inbox

Keep your e-mail password safe. People who know your password can read your e-mail and even send e-mails pretending to be you! Change your password every few months. **Delete** any messages that contain private information.

Often, any Web site you join will send you an e-mail when you sign up. These e-mails could

Your e-mails should be safe if you have a strong password. E-mail is a great way to talk to friends and family. Do not send e-mails filled with private information, though.

contain information about your user name. This is why it is important to keep different passwords for every account you have. If someone can access your e-mail, he can learn a lot about the different places you go online. If you use the same password all over the Internet, someone could log in to all of the sites you use as you. If you think someone is reading your e-mail, change your password right away.

Going Wireless

Cell phones, laptops, and tablets can connect to the Internet wirelessly. That means that they do not have to be physically plugged into the source of the Internet. They connect over the air. When you connect to a wireless network, though, you need to make sure it is secure. In your home, protect your network with a password. This way, no one outside your home can use your Internet connection. If someone used your connection to do bad things online, it could be traced back to your household. Also, with the right know-how, people can steal information from computers on unprotected networks. Your family should decide on a strong password for your home connection.

Be aware of your connection when you are using a cell phone, tablet, or laptop in a public place. Coffee shops and libraries often have free wireless Internet. Remember, this is an open connection and so it is not password protected. Never surf on sensitive sites, like e-mail or banks, from public places because your information might not be secure from prying eyes.

Spam and Phishing Schemes

Spam messages are e-mails that offer you things you did not ask for and do not need. Delete these messages without opening them. Many e-mail programs have built-in filters that block spam and junk mail.

Phishing schemes are e-mails that use lies to trick you. They may look like e-mails from a trustworthy place. However, they ask you to send personal information that can be used to steal from you. Sometimes they may even seem like a letter from a real person who needs your help. The person may ask you for money. **Ignore** these e-mails and never reply to them.

A good rule is to open e-mails only from people you know and trust. If an e-mail has an **attachment**, ask an adult before opening it.

Spam is mail sent to mislead or trick you into thinking it is from someone you know. Usually, the message tries to get you to buy something. Sometimes it tries to trick you into sharing user names and passwords.

Spying on You

Web browsers store **cookies** on computers. These are not baked treats, but packets of information. Cookies store settings, passwords, or other **data**. Cookies also let Web sites know what other places you visit. You cannot turn off cookies. However, you can delete cookies. Settings to delete cookies can be found in your browser **preferences**.

Some sites use software called **spyware** to track your Internet use. Companies generally use this data to try to sell you things. Some spyware can track the keys you type on your keyboard. Thieves use spyware to try to steal passwords. Avoid spyware by not downloading unknown applications. The Mac App Store or CNET are safe places to download software. Always talk to an adult before downloading any new apps.

Web sites often track your activity. Ask a librarian or teacher how to delete cookies from school and library computers.

Avoiding Predators

The Internet can be a great place to learn and have fun, but there are some people who use the Internet to harm children. These people are known as online predators. They may pretend to be your age to become your friend. If a stranger tries to **contact** you in a chat room, on a message board, or by e-mail, do not answer. If somebody asks you to send pictures of yourself or sends you pictures, tell an adult. Online predators break the law. An adult may need to call the police.

Do not let the predator make you feel guilty. The online predator is the one who has done something wrong. Remember, if a predator sends you a message, it is not your fault.

If you get a message from an online predator, tell an adult. You might feel scared or alone. It is important to get help to deal with a predator.

Erasing Your Data

You might find someday that something has been posted about you on the Internet. The information might be there because you made a mistake and put it online. A friend may have made a bad choice and posted your photo, phone number, or e-mail address. Bullies also

Protect the privacy of your friends, too. Do not write or post anything about anyone else without asking first. Talk to your friends about privacy online.

sometimes put other people's information online on purpose.

Sometimes you can delete a post or comment or ask the friend who posted it to delete the information. If it cannot be deleted, talk to an adult, such as a parent or teacher. An adult may have to contact the site to have the information taken down. Act fast and fix the problem. Do not be scared or ignore it. That information may not go away by itself.

Privacy on Social Networks

Social networks are a fun way to connect with your friends and family online. Many social networks allow you to create a profile about yourself. You can also post photos and status updates about what you are doing. Be smart when posting to social networks. Never reveal private information in your profile, like your full name, e-mail address, phone number, or where you live. Do not post pictures of yourself or friends for everyone to see. Ask friends to check with you before posting photos. Sit down with an adult and review the privacy settings on your profile. Make sure the only people who can see your profile are people you know. Do not ever give a friend your user name and password. This information is only yours. If a friend finds out a password, change it right away.

Safety Tips

- Make a list of personal information with a parent so that you will know what to keep private.

- Find a safe spot in which to hide your passwords. Your backpack is not safe enough!

- Never click on links that offer you money or prizes.

- Set up your e-mail to receive messages only from people who are in your address book.

- Bookmark safe sites and clear cookies from your browser regularly.

- Make a list of "Online Dos and Don'ts" to hang near your computer.

- Put a password on your phone so no one can use it but you.

- Use different passwords for different sites.

- Talk to a parent about installing antispyware software on your computer.

- Ask your friends not to post pictures or information about you online.

attachment (uh-TACH-mint) An extra part of an e-mail, such as a photo or text document, that you must click on to open.

blog (BLOG) A Web site where people share thoughts and facts.

contact (KON-takt) To talk or meet with a person.

cookies (KU-keez) Text files that Web browsers store.

data (DAY-tuh) Facts.

delete (dih-LEET) To erase or get rid of totally.

identity (EYE-dent-ih-tee) Who someone is.

ignore (ig-NOR) To pay no attention to something.

information (in-fer-MAY-shun) Knowledge or facts.

password (PAS-wurd) A secret combination of letters or numbers that lets people enter something, like a Web site.

preferences (PREH-fernts-ez) Things people choose about a computer's setup.

profiles (PRO-fylz) On social networks, profiles are pages that describe users' interests and personalities.

protect (pruh-TEKT) To keep safe.

screen name (SKREEN NAYM) A name someone uses online.

social networks (SO-shul net-WERKS) Web sites where people connect with friends and family.

spyware (SPY-wayr) Computer software that secretly collects user information.

symbols (SIM-bulz) Objects or pictures that stand for other things.

Index

A
adult(s), 5, 10, 14, 16, 18, 21

C
cell phone(s), 5–6, 13
computer(s), 5–6, 13, 16, 22
cookies, 16, 22

E
e-mail(s), 5–6, 12–14, 18, 20–21, 22

H
home, 5, 13

I
identity, 5
information, 4–6, 8, 10, 12–14, 16, 20–22

Internet, 4–5, 10, 13, 16, 18, 20

L
laptop(s), 5, 13
list, 5, 22

M
Mac App Store, 16
message(s), 12, 14, 18, 22
mobile devices, 5

N
name, 5–6, 13, 21

P
password(s), 6, 12–13, 16, 21–22
phone(s), 5–6, 13, 22

preferences, 16
profile(s), 5, 21

R
reminder, 5

S
screen name, 6
social network(s), 8, 10, 21
spyware, 16
stranger, 18
symbols, 6

T
topics, 4

W
Web site(s), 5–6, 8, 10, 12–13, 16, 21–22

Web Sites

Due to the changing nature of Internet links, PowerKids Press has developed an online list of Web sites related to the subject of this book. This site is updated regularly. Please use this link to access the list:

www.powerkidslinks.com/cyber/privacy